COLLEEN J. PALLAMARY

* Advance Praise for Scammunition *

Scammunition is a spot-on supplier of serious information for those of us who trust too much. Colleen Pallamary has been there, done that and bought the T-shirt . . . but she did not buy into the lies, deceit and treachery inherent in the countless scams that threaten us on a daily basis. Better still, she speaks to us with an authority earned through her association with the Florida Attorney General's Office, combined with years of experience and her intuitive knowledge of things, places and people. As a retired cop, I can see a place for her book on every consumer's and every cop's bookshelf.

-- Richard Craig Anderson, author of Rivers of Belief and Ready Room - A Site for Cops and Writers

Colleen has done an excellent job of identifying the most frequent ways that consumers are separated from their money! Her easy to read description of ways to potentially lose your money and the simple steps you should take to avoid becoming a victim should be a must read for everyone. A good read packed with easy to understand scam prevention tips.

-- Don Ravenna President, Seniors vs. Crime, Inc.

This book is a tool for both caregivers and the cared for and is first line protection for crimes against vulnerable people who can't say no.

-- Robert Simpson, Retired Florida Assistant State Attorney

A must read for all ages. Very insightful. Will make you take a closer look at possible scam artists."

-- Robert and Angela McElroy, Horse Trainers, Ocala Fl .

This book is a must read for those who are concerned about the plight of the elderly in this country.

-- Zach Hudson, CNN Hero 2012

Knowledge is ammunition and the world is full of wolves. Colleen Pallamary provides an arsenal of information to help folks hunt the wolves that would prey on the trust of our good intentions. Reputable businesses, or deals, should never have a problem providing you verifiable sources and contacts. Trust is earned and what you've earned should never be trusted to someone who is not willing to earn that trust with as much hard work as you did to earn the money to pay them. What a resource.

-- Wes Albers has more than a quarter century of experience in law enforcement and security. He is the author of Black & White from Zova Books.

Scammunition

How to Protect Yourself From Con Artists:
A Guide for Baby Boomers and Beyond

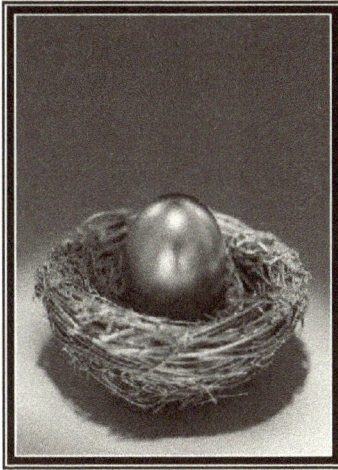

by

Colleen J. Pallamary

PP

Pallamary Publishing

COLLEEN J. PALLAMARY

Pallamary Publishing
Ocala, FL
www.pallamarypublishing.com

First published by Pallamary Publishing September 19, 2012

ISBN 10: 061569702X (sc)
ISBN 13: 978-0615697024 (sc)
Printed in the United States of America
North Charleston, South Carolina

This book is printed on acid-free paper made from 30% post-consumer waste recycled material.

Library of Congress Control Number: 2012917112

Book Jacket Design: Matthew J. Pallamary / San Diego CA
Cover Photograph: Courtesy of CreateSpace

This book is dedicated to Colleen Joan Kennedy

My Wonderful Mom

CONTENTS

PART 2:   WHEN CALLER I.D. DOESN'T HELP

PART 3: COMPUTER CONS AND CONSEQUENCES

SCAMMUNITION

COLLEEN J. PALLAMARY

ACKNOWLEDGEMENTS

The author would like to thank the Florida Attorney General's Office and the Seniors vs. Crime Project for giving me the opportunity to help victims of scams. Although I no longer volunteer with SVC, I would like to acknowledge the following people who assisted me in my efforts to help citizens in our community. My colleagues Rita Knopf, Tony Pace, and Maryellen Rivers volunteered their time and worked tirelessly to assist community members in their skirmishes with scammers. Thanks to them for sharing their wisdom and time.

Thanks also to others who have been supportive in other aspects of my life including Polly Bee, Karen and Danny Mayer, Lynne Engel-Holmes and her daughters Crystal and Rachael. Each has inspired me with their willingness to believe in me and what I am doing.

Thank you to my children, Michelle Woodward, MaryAnne Buckley, and Carl Peterson III.

Last, but not least, to my mother, Colleen J. Kennedy, who now rests with angels and dances with butterflies, my eternal thanks for her unconditional love and for always showing me that "something of value" can never be measured in numerical terms.

FOREWORD

I am the oldest of four children raised by a wonderful mother, a single parent who did her best with what she had. None of us had much in the way of material goods but we were loved and shared a common bond of togetherness in the face of adversity. My Mom taught me at an early age that the most important things in life, like honesty and integrity, don't cost a thing and that giving and keeping my word was more valuable than anything else I could offer. It is a principle I live by to this day.

My Mom also taught me to respect my elders. I did, still do and now I am one! I'm not sure what happens when you get older, other than the obvious, and I've tried to figure out what makes some people susceptible to the schemes and dreams of scam artists and cons. There are no neon signs flashing "potential victims" or bull's eyes painted on our backs yet millions of people become targets every day and the scam phenomena flourishes in the fertile fields of imaginative minds. I personally became aware of the extensive damage caused by con artists when I volunteered as office manager with the Seniors vs. Crime Project, a special project of the Florida Attorney General's Office.

For four years my staff and I worked on hundreds of cases ranging from deceptive salespeople misrepresenting products to checking on a pair of lowlifes stalking elderly people each month when Social Security checks were due to try to get them to buy meat from a cooler in the back of a rusted pickup truck . Food pitches for "great savings", "reduced prices" and "limited time offers" are geared towards hungry senior citizens trying to get by with very little income and no help from family members. Unfortunately, not all scam victims have favorable outcomes so I lectured, gave workshops, and wrote a monthly column to educate readers and community groups about the potential dangers we all face as consumers. As Benjamin Franklin once said, "An ounce of prevention is worth a pound of cure" and I believe that applies here.

Although I no longer work with that particular project, I continue to help others and stay informed about scams. I have written **Scammunition** as a guide. It is not my intent to make anyone frightened or paranoid and it is not legal advice, nor is it meant to replace it. I am simply sharing some of the knowledge I have gained through years of experience so that others can gain a new perspective on how and why they need to learn about scams. **Scammunition** is the result of my efforts and represents my pro-active stance against scumbags. Times have certainly changed since I was a teenager, but my heartfelt beliefs in honesty, integrity, and respect haven't. I'm here to help. You have my word!

New Updates! The world is changing at a rapid pace and scammers still prey on innocent people. I have updated this edition with additional tips and hints in keeping with the ever-evolving times and my mission remains the same – to help others whenever and wherever I can!

Colleen J. Pallamary   March 2021

INTRODUCTION

Gone are the days when a person's word or handshake was all that was needed to finalize a business deal. It's human nature to trust. We learn at an early age that our best friend is someone we can count on and confide in. We want to believe that people are inherently good and have our best interests at heart. But what happens when that friend asks for a loan to start a new business then leaves town with all your money, never to be heard from again? How about the businessman with a great reputation who makes a proposal, takes a down payment, and never shows up to do any work? Consider the strange emails filling inboxes with promises of infinite wealth and the chance to connect with long-lost relatives from foreign lands. These and many other scenarios are playing out across the United States and the world at an alarming rate.

History is full of dishonest dealings. In the 1980's, investment schemes dominated the news, ruining lives with lies and deceit. In the 1880's things weren't much different. Immeasurable harm and senseless deaths occurred when Native Americans were slaughtered and forced off land that was rightfully theirs, while fraudulent land scams were pushed on an unsuspecting public as pioneers moved westward in search of new lives.

Scams and cons have changed through the decades, keeping up with the huge technological strides made during the last century. Information that was once transported by Pony Express is now sent via email programs like Outlook Express. Unfortunately, communication advances have inadvertently allowed cybercrimes to become more prominent in everyone's lives. Transactions that were once considered safe and protected are now breeding grounds for illegal activities. Self-preservation has taken on a whole new meaning and self-defense is no longer just physical.

Thieves, con artists, and scammers come in all shapes and sizes including invisible ones living in cyberspace as so-called "friends". Countless bank and credit card accounts have been hijacked online and savings accrued over decades of hard work have been wiped out in seconds by devious cons. Boomers relying on retirement accounts and 401 k plans can kiss their futures goodbye if their funds disappear. Heartless hackers don't care. Their games are played with phones, emails, and a simple plan. Feeling stupid and used, many consumers remain silent and the rip-offs go unreported. No one is immune.

It's time once again for the dreaded word "homework" to creep back into your vocabulary. Arm yourself with knowledge and learn some tricks of the scam prevention trade. If you've been scammed you are not alone. There is help available; you just need to know where to look. **Scammunition** is where to start. Please note: Some URLS and contact information may change. It is correct as of this writing.

PART 1

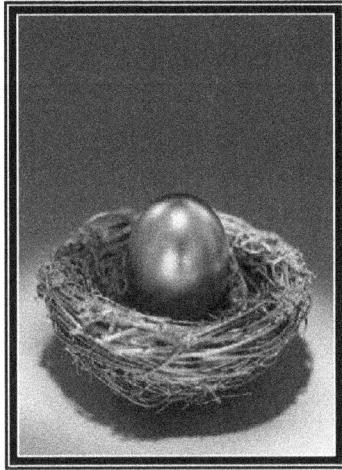

ONE – ON – ONE TRANSACTIONS

COLLEEN J. PALLAMARY

ONE

FIRST STEPS

How to Initiate a Complaint

Have you ever purchased a product that didn't meet your expectations or didn't do what it claimed to do? Maybe it was smaller than it looked in an ad or perhaps it didn't work at all. A common complaint isn't necessarily a scam, but it has to do with deceptive advertising and the failure to properly disclose all of the details of a transaction prior to purchase.

Suppose John Smith orders a product (we'll call it "The Wheeler Dealer Thing") after seeing it on television. The offer states that if you act now, you can get two "Wheeler Dealer Things" for the price of one. He picks up the phone, punches all the buttons, and orders two. Imagine his surprise when he gets the bill and it's more than the price stated in the "special offer". In addition, the "Wheeler Dealer Things" were very cheaply made and fell apart when used for the first time. He calls the company to inquire about the additional charges and is informed that even though the second product was free, he still has to pay additional shipping and handling fees and taxes on the purchase. The representative explains that by purchasing their product he automatically agreed to the charges because their fees were flashed on the screen. He watches for the commercial that night and in letters too small to read and with no voiceover, the charges were listed. While technically the company was right, it's a deceptive way to conduct business and the ads have since changed. However, it is worth noting this particular issue because the smallest details are the ones that may need the most attention. Here are some consumer facts.

Within the U.S., each state has enacted regulatory codes, laws, and statutes with the intention of protecting consumers. Civil negotiations and effective resolutions may be the ultimate goals, but part of the problem is figuring out the first steps to take when making a legitimate complaint. There are times when the best resource for information may be your local phone book. Do you have issues with a contractor? Call the local building department. Are you having problems with defective workmanship? Start local and work your way up to the state level. Product not as advertised? Notify the company.

Many people have computers, but disabled, homebound people may only have a pen and paper to use while others may not even have a phone. Prior to the Internet, most complaints were either handled by phone, mail, or in person. Nowadays most companies have online complaint forms that allow consumers to communicate with the touch of a button. The same rules apply no matter which method is used and getting to the point is the goal.

Whether speaking or writing, be as brief and concise as possible. Long, detailed stories waste time and may cloud the issue for the person you are complaining to. State your problem as soon as possible and explain what type of resolution you seek. Don't add unnecessary details such as "It was a cold day and I woke up with a headache. I hate cold days. They always make me feel grouchy etc., etc., etc." An example of a complaint letter might be as follows:

Dear Manager: (One hint here. If possible call and ask for the manager's/supervisor's name. Personalizing your letter lets you know you are dealing with a person and vice versa. The recipient knows the complaint is directed to their attention and is more apt to read it all the way through.).

On (insert date) I purchased two "Wheeler Dealer Things" from your company ad on TV. I charged it to my XXX charge account (if applicable change payment method such as paid cash/used debit card etc.). After using your products for a day, they fell apart. Your policy states that you have a 30 day money back guarantee (or whatever the policy may be). I would like a full refund. Enclosed please find a copy of my dated receipt. If you have any questions I can be reached at 000-000-0000.

Sincerely,

John Smith

Depending on the complaint, it may take several days or weeks to get a response. If you don't hear back within a reasonable amount of time, send another letter with a notation that it's a second request. Some businesses prefer to call you. Be sure to document conversations by making note of the date and time of the call, the contact person you spoke with, and a brief description of the conversation.

Another way to resolve a complaint is to call a company's corporate office. Check the company's website online for their contact info. Make sure you are on a legitimate site before calling. Scammers use a technique called "spoofing" to trick folks into believing they are on a corporate site when , in reality, it is a fake site designed to steal your personal info. Use caution when searching. It may take several minutes to reach the right person, but the problem might be solved quickly. Be patient and polite. The right approach can help everyone.

Simple and To The Point

TWO

DON'T HIRE A *CON* - TRACTOR

Advice on Hiring Contractors

Choosing a contractor isn't easy, nor should it be. Your time, money, and projects are all at stake. Slick ads, business cards, and telephone directories list a variety of services while sales brochures and coupons offer discounts and payment plans fit for every budget. The offers may help, but they don't disclose the important details about the person you want to hire including those who invent stories and excuses to scam you out of your money. Rather than call them contractors, let's classify them as CONtractors.

Consider a scenario with a house painter. He does a wonderful job painting the exterior of a home in a senior community. He and his crew complete the job in record time and then knock on doors and offer special deals to other homeowners in the area using the newly painted house as a reference. Several people sign contracts, pick paint colors, and make down payments to the friendly business owner. Several months later angry homeowners share a common problem: no paint, no painters, and no recourse because the CONtractor disappeared with everyone's money and moved on to another county for a repeat performance. Prepaid cell phones are tossed in the trash and there is no way to track the scam artist team.

Be leery of sales sob stories. Pleas for extra money to pay for gas, tires, and shoes for children are actually ways to rip you off. Demands for huge down payments and strange tales that don't sound logical are warning signs. If something sounds too good to be true, it probably is. Always get at least three estimates for a job. Make sure the business name, address, license number and phone numbers are all on the company paperwork and never pay in full before a job is started. Ask for proof of insurance. An estimated start and completion date should be included in a work order and don't sign a contract until you have read it. Never pay with cash! It can't be tracked. Credit cards and checks may afford some protection against fraudulent acts.

Pulling permits is another area where unlicensed CONtractors may try to take advantage of unsuspecting clients. Permits are necessary for certain jobs such as enlarging, repairing, or changing the occupancy of a building or structure. They are not needed for projects like valve and faucet repairs or painting or replacing carpets. For a complete list of services that require permits call the local building department in your area. Be aware that in most states, if you pull a permit in YOUR name and an issue arises, YOU are listed as the contractor and YOU are responsible for solving any problems. The actual person you hired is then considered a subcontractor who is working under your direction and matters can get very complicated from there especially in terms of liabilities. Add some scheming cronies to the mix and you'll have a recipe for ruin. Check your local regulations before taking any steps.

General contractors oversee an entire project while subcontractors do specialized work such as electrical or plumbing projects. Every person hired to work should be licensed and insured. To verify state licenses, check local phone listings for the proper authorities. Many states offer online inquiries regarding licensing issues. Proof of insurance, also known as certificates of liability insurance, should be reviewed carefully and a simple phone call to the agent or insurance company can verify coverage.

In any business deal everyone has a share of responsibility. If an adequate job has been performed, payment must be made. If there are problems with the finished product, there are protocols to follow. It's not enough to accept deals at face value or to rely on a handshake. There are too many loopholes and discrepancies for seasoned con artists to slip through and use to their advantage. Be a smart consumer and take nothing for granted. Inquire before you hire and your part of the job is done.

Acceptable Estimate

John Smith Company
123 Main St.
Anytown USA 12345
555-555-5555
License # 111111

Materials and Labor $XXXX.XX

Estimated Start Date   10/30/2018

Estimated Completion   11/15/2018

Down Payment of 20% Credit cards and checks accepted.

Balance Due Upon Completion

Not Acceptable

Joe Jones
Cell 555-555-5555

Materials and Labor
Not sure

Estimated Start Date
End of winter

Estimated Completion
Sometime in summer

Down Payment of 50%
Cash only

Balance Due
Week before finished

THREE

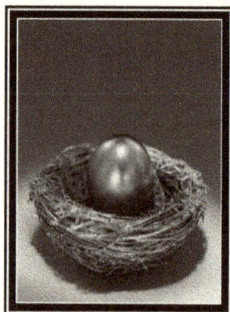

CHECK IT OUT

Insurance Coverage: Who Needs it and Why

Insurance can be a controversial subject. Who needs it? Who wants it? What's it for? As a former insurance customer service rep I understand the confusion. No matter how you feel about it, the important thing to remember is that you need protection when hiring contractors. By insisting on seeing proof of insurance from potential employees, YOU take control of the working environment and establish safety guidelines.

Reputable businesses purchase commercial liability insurance policies. A slick salesperson may show you a printed document called an "Insurance Binder" and claim that it is an insurance policy. Read it carefully! The term "binder" means a temporary policy, valid for 30-90 days until an actual policy is issued. A binder is NOT proof of commercial liability insurance. It is issued by the insurance company when an initial down payment is made by the person purchasing coverage. The actual form used as evidence of coverage is called a "Certificate of Liability Insurance" and is issued by the insurance agent on behalf of the insurance company. The forms look alike so pay attention to details. On the left side of the form the word "Producer" means the insurance AGENT and beneath that the word "Insured" is where the business name should be listed. Directly across from the business name is the name of the insurance COMPANY, not to be confused with the agent. Both, however, can verify coverage. Throughout the form the effective dates of the policy and various limits of liability are listed. At the bottom of the form is a section called "Certificate Holder" and this is where your name or business should be listed. It is also where your homework begins.

DO NOT ASSUME COVERAGE IS VALID!

Just because someone provides you with a copy of a certificate, it does NOT mean they have insurance. Some people pay a minimum down payment, get a certificate, and then never pay their premium. The policy is cancelled and they intentionally present the invalid certificate to unsuspecting clients who accept it as proof of coverage. Insurance agents try to contact certificate holders (you, if you are listed) about the cancellation, but it may be too late. As a consumer you can make a request for a certificate to be sent directly to your home. The insured person (the one you are hiring) has to notify the agent and the agent sends it out. You can then check further by calling the agent (producer) yourself to verify coverage.

Commercial liability insurance serves a dual purpose. Coverage is purchased to protect business owners in case their employees cause damage to a client's property or if they cause injury to others. It can also cover the business property and vehicles as well. Some business owners opt to purchase package policies and others opt to buy separate coverages depending on their needs. Workers comp laws vary from state to state and it's an important consideration when hiring someone to work on your property. Individual owners who are lone employees may not need it.

If you take the time to call for any type of service, spend a few moments to check out the small print. Valid insurance protects everyone involved in a project, especially you!

Example of Binder/Temporary Policy/Valid 30 – 90 Days

Example of Certificate of Liability Insurance

FOUR

PLEASE AND THANK YOU

Don't Forget Your Manners

Contracts have certain requirements. Signatures, dates, and payment information are a few of the details necessary in any negotiation. Many businesses and clients don't realize that each agreement contains an unspoken, unwritten obligation to be polite and professional with each other AFTER a contract is signed. Here are some thoughts.

SELLER SUGGESTIONS:

Try to understand the frustration and anger clients feel while sitting at home waiting for promised calls that never come. Many times people rearrange their entire schedules in order to speak with you. Perhaps a customer has a question about your service or needs to make a change to an existing plan. Maybe they have misunderstood a key element in a business proposal or just need reassurance that they haven't been forgotten. After all, people feel valued BEFORE signing a contract; their status shouldn't change once they sign on the dotted line. One return call from a courteous person can generate more business for you just by word of mouth and goodwill. Good communication is vital for any transaction.

PURCHASER POINTS:

On the other hand, customers need to be patient and reasonable. If someone from a company tells you they will call next week, please don't complain at 9:01 A.M. on Monday morning because they haven't called yet. The week has barely begun! Some businesses call during certain hours out of respect for customers and avoid early morning or evening calls. The person you want to speak to may be out of the area for the day or might be in a "dead zone" where cell phones have no service. Sometimes a game of telephone tag can resolve an issue when each party leaves the other messages.

Both sides should stop and think of any unforeseen circumstances that could affect a situation. Try to understand some delays can't be helped and are beyond anyone's control. For example, adverse weather conditions can affect the completion of an outdoor project. Don't expect a landscaping company to work in a torrential downpour even if you do have an appointment and an anticipated completion date. Sellers should notify clients of any changes as soon as possible. If you are delayed for some reason, let them know. Sitting around waiting for discourteous people who can't take a moment to make a quick call to say they are running late can cause hard feelings.

Consideration works both ways in any relationship, especially in business dealings. Consumers and vendors can work together to make transactions run smoothly and any difficulties or issues can be worked out in a calm and civil manner. If need be, contact a manager or supervisor to assist. Sometimes an objective observer can offer a whole new perspective on a problem that hasn't been thought of before. Everyone can benefit by being courteous and respectful. "Please" and "thank you" go a long way towards job satisfaction for both sides.

Another View of Manners

```
        T
        H
    PLEASE
        N
        K
    CUSTOMER
            E
            F
        MORE
            R
        SALES
              O   P
              A   L
          EVERYONE
                  A
                  S
                  E
```

FIVE

WAIT A MINUTE

Spring Cleaning Safeguards

Sixty seconds is all it takes to tap out a text and send it, make a cup of tea, or read a paragraph in a favorite magazine. It's also plenty of time to perform a personalized scam prevention program from the comfort of your easy chair at home. Whether dining out, spring cleaning closets, or having a yard sale, a minute of your time can save you years of stress and confusion. Spend a few moments paying attention to small details and reap huge rewards. Here's how.

CASH OR DEBIT: Dinner was wonderful, the service great, and your empty dessert plate is on its way to a sudsy sauna. The check arrives, you skim over the figures and sign your name, leaving a generous cash tip on the table. The receipt, like your meal, becomes a distant memory and is soon forgotten. Your bank statement arrives and it goes in a drawer with the rest of the mail to be opened later at a more convenient time. However, unbeknownst to you and hundreds of others, some unscrupulous businesses are actually ADDING money onto your signed debit slip and pocketing the difference! They secretly add an additional amount as a tip even if you've already left one on the table. Take a moment and check bank statements. Compare the amounts that are debited to your actual receipts. If you are a victim of this type of scam, return to the restaurant, speak with a manager, and, if not satisfied, contact the corporate offices. In the meantime, if you still pay for meals with your debit card and prefer to leave a cash gratuity, write directly on the receipt "cash on table" or "tip on table". It will help prevent unauthorized deductions.

NEED FOR GREED: Your favorite author has just released a new book and the bookstore is having a sale. You purchase the novel with your charge card and finally carve out a block of time to read. The story is captivating, the characters real, and reluctantly you put the book down using your credit card receipt as a bookmark. Months pass and it's time for your annual spring-cleaning routine. Like many people, rather than toss out usable items, you might choose to donate books and clothing to favorite charitable organizations or have a yard sale. Don't forget to check pages and pockets for personal information! Credit card receipts can have enough information for identity theft and illegal charges. A long forgotten bill or note crumpled inside an old pocket may resurface as a new account under a stranger's name. Before donating or selling personal property, take it, shake it, and don't let anyone fake it with your good name and credit.

SAFE AND SECURE: We live in a world of instant gratification. Microwave ovens heat food in seconds, remote controls switch channels in the blink of an eye, and savvy scammers strike with precision timing. When practiced regularly, spending a few moments taking precautions can easily become routine. There are no manuals for common sense and no reason why we can't rely on ourselves for the best protection available. It only takes a minute.

It Takes Just A Minute

SIX

ARE YOU EXPERIENCED?

Hiring Competent Caregivers

Baby Boomers looking forward to retirement are facing some unexpected dilemmas. Adult children are flocking back home and aging parents may require attention and assistance with everyday needs. Medical and health issues can strike loved ones and there may be occasion to hire someone to provide services in a home setting. I cared for my Mom for 5 years as she bravely battled colon cancer, but others may not be able to do that and have to consider different options. Hiring a caregiver can be a daunting task and it is crucial to do some research and make informed decisions before the hiring process begins. There are several types of homecare, licensing requirements, and agencies that employ caregivers. Defining your specific needs is a good place to begin.

There are no federal regulations governing home care services. Each state is responsible for setting up guidelines for each level of care and consumers often don't know the difference. For example, a homemaker can prepare meals, shop, and perform household chores. A companion spends time with clients and engages them in various activities such as visiting friends, going to the doctor, or simply watching a movie together. Many homemaker / companions work as independent contractors and do not report to any agencies. On the other hand, home health aides and certified nursing assistants can provide hands-on care including bathing, grooming, and help with dressing. They are monitored by their employing agency. If a person is under a physician's care, a registered nurse may be hired and a licensed agency will supervise that care, too.

Licensing requirements for each level of care varies from state to state and background checks can make the difference between hiring a competent caregiver or a clever con. Local law enforcement agencies can provide you with options for background checks, and in some states like Florida, court records and inmate histories are readily available online. Ask the potential employee about their training and experience. Do they know CPR and First Aid? How long have they been working in their particular position. Do they have references? Check with the Consumer Services Division of your state's Attorney General's office to see what qualifications are required for each level of care and then check to be sure the person is actually licensed. Pay particular attention to the caregiver's interactions with your loved one. If anyone is uncomfortable on either side, send the potential employee on their way.

Vulnerable people may be unaware of what is going on around them, especially when ill. They are often reluctant to complain, and, in some instances, actually nurture an emotional bond with a particular caregiver. It is wise to remain observant when allowing someone else into your life and the life of your loved ones. Some tell-tale signs of scam activity might include unusual bank account transactions, missing valuables, the addition of a caregiver's name on accounts, and an increase in credit card activity with no visible evidence of purchases. For more tips and ideas contact the Administration on Aging at **1-202-401-4634** or visit their website at www.acl.gov. Another resource for referrals and information is Eldercare Locator, **1-800-677-1116**, or visit www.eldercare.acl.gov. It is up to consumers to be prepared before making important decisions. Care giving works both ways when it comes to loved ones and their well-being.

Types of Home Care Providers

- Homemaker

- Companion

- Home Health Aide

- CNA (Certified Nursing Assistant)

- LPN (Licensed Practical Nurse)

- RN (Registered Nurse)

Check Licensing Requirements in Your State!

- Know who you are hiring and why

- Household chores

- Personal care

- Medical issues

Warning Signs and Questionable Behavior

- Numerous checks made out to cash

- Unpaid bills

- Strange signatures on important papers

- Missing personal effects

- Expensive gifts to caregiver

SEVEN

LAST RIGHTS?

The Funeral Rule and What It Does

Most of us don't relate the concept of undercover work to our shopping needs. The term is usually associated with novels, movies, and news reports of drug-busting government agencies assigned to catch the bad guys and bring them to justice. There is one industry covered by federal law that actually uses undercover agents in an effort to protect vulnerable consumers from financial harm. The Federal Trade Commission enforces "The Funeral Rule", a regulation enacted in 1984 that provides specific guidelines for funeral homes and directors to follow when dealing with grief-stricken clients. Between 2015 and 2016, investigators found over 30 violations of the Funeral Rule in nine states for failure to disclose price lists. First time offenders are offered special training via the Funeral Rule Offender's Program which includes safeguards to ensure compliance with the rules. Caskets, price lists, and package deals are a few of the areas routinely inspected by agents and they warrant our attention as well.

Making funeral arrangements is never easy, especially if no pre-planning is involved. Unscrupulous funeral directors use several deceptive tactics. Consider choosing a casket. During the very emotional process of trying to decide where to place a loved one, the most expensive caskets are presented first. The hope is that the grieving person will opt for the most expensive model instead of a lower priced one. Some funeral homes actually hide the less expensive caskets in the basement and others have been known to paint them unattractive colors in an effort to divert attention away from the lower price. Another tactic is adding an additional charge for special gaskets which claim to preserve and protect the deceased remains for a prolonged period of time. There simply is no way to accomplish that with any feature on a casket. In addition, most people are unaware that they can purchase a casket or urn elsewhere and use it at any funeral home free of charge.

Funeral directors are obligated by law to provide prospective clients with a price list BEFORE actually showing any items or explaining any services. There are certain basic fees that must be paid to the funeral director and staff such as planning the actual funeral, obtaining any permits that may be required, sheltering the remains, and costs for death certificates to name a few. Prices vary from state to state and if a local or state law has a specific requirement regarding the purchase of a certain item, information about the law and price of the required good/service must be included on the list.

At first glance package deals might seem to be the most economical, but do you need all of the goods and services that are listed? If cremation and direct burial are your options, why incur fees for embalming when it's not necessary? Do you need a two-day viewing or is an hour sufficient? Clergy, music, and additional staff may be available in a package but do you need them? Review price lists carefully so you don't purchase what you don't need and be sure to get a written itemized statement before paying any fees.

Nowadays folks might want to consider a Digital Estate Plan outlining preferences for social media accounts, websites, retail, and email accounts. A Digital Executor can carry out instructions for closing or memorializing a deceased persons digital media. Check with individual websites for clarifications. List passwords, account numbers, and other pertinent info and keep in a safe place.

Most funeral directors are caring and compassionate licensed professionals who follow a Code of Professional Conduct. They know that their specialized services may not be familiar to mourners and take great care to explain and assist with the decision-making process. For more information contact your state or local consumer protection agency or visit www.FTC.gov/funerals .You and your loved ones will rest easy knowing you were able to protect their last rights.

Pricing Checklist Suggestions from FTC

"Simple" disposition of the remains:	
Immediate burial	
Immediate cremation	
If the cremation process is extra, how much is it?	
Donation of the body to a medical school or hospital	
"Traditional," full-service burial or cremation:	
Basic services fee for the funeral director and staff	
Pickup of body	
Embalming	
Other preparation of body	
Least expensive casket	
Description, including model #	
Outer Burial Container (vault)	
Description	
Visitation/viewing — staff and facilities	
Funeral or memorial service — staff and facilities	
Graveside service, including staff and equipment	
Hearse	
Other vehicles	
Total	
Other Services:	
Forwarding body to another funeral home	
Receiving body from another funeral home	
Other Services:	
Cost of lot or crypt (if you don't already own one)	
Perpetual care	
Opening and closing the grave or crypt	
Grave liner, if required	
Marker/monument (including setup)	

PART 2

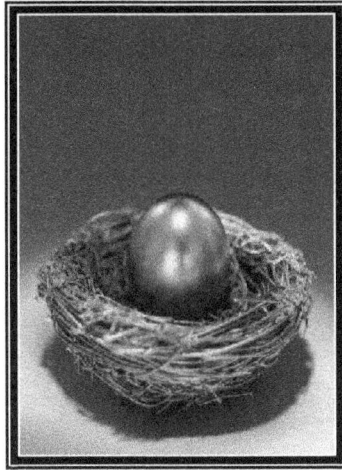

WHEN CALLER ID DOESN'T HELP

EIGHT

GOOD BUY OR GOOD BYE?

Safe Travels

Excitement, adventure, foreign locales – the lure of travel is irresistible to many people. Brochures and magazines beckon readers to visit sun-kissed islands and white-tipped mountains for fun and relaxation and online offers seem too good to pass up. Dishonest telemarketers are skilled at using high pressure sales tactics when pitching travel offers and emails offering incentives to become a travel agent sound like fun. Whether by phone or on the computer, "special discounts" and "limited time deals" demanding immediate payment should raise red flags. Don't wave your credit card in response until you've investigated the unbelievable bargains.

Offers to travel are sometimes wrapped in packages designed to mask the real intent. Excited voices inform you that you've won a vacation but have to claim it immediately or a bargain deal is available for the next half hour only. The offers can be as outlandish as the cost! Never purchase tickets without a written contract and don't pay with cash! Scammers offer to use couriers to collect payments in exchange for a promise to send the necessary paperwork once they receive your money. The ruse allows them to avoid any charges of mail fraud if they are caught taking your money under false pretenses. Another tactic is to ask you to pay by credit card more than 60 days in advance of your trip because that's the time limit for disputing any questionable charges. Folks are then left with nowhere to go, both literally and figuratively.

Joining a travel club or becoming a travel agent may be appealing to some people, but the details and incentives need to be checked with care. Instructional programs to become a travel agent can cost thousands of dollars and hidden fees can be added to travel club deals. Free trips and cruises can be riddled with problems once passengers begin their journeys. Dismayed clients can find themselves in poor accommodations and upgrades, if available, cost the same as that of other competitors. Calls to toll-free numbers go unanswered and messages aren't returned. Meanwhile, scammers are on a trip of their own while stranded travelers are stuck with no recourse, no refunds, and, in some instances, no way to get home.

Recently popular travel site Airbnb has received complaints from consumers who have made reservations for travel accommodations only to find their money missing and their plans destroyed. Airbnb advises everyone to read their safety precautions and follow their specific instructions for payments. Their secure website is https://www.airbnb.com.

There are several options available for people planning a trip. Use an agent or a reputable website. State consumer protection agencies can verify registration information for any business. Know the lingo used in ads and beware of the lack of details in travel offers. Locally, your nearby travel agent may have information on training opportunities or you may contact the American Society of Travel Agents, an organization of professional travel agents with decades of experience in the industry. Visit their website at www.asta.org for tips. For international travel visit the U.S. Dept. of State site at www.travel.state.gov .

Vacations are an investment. Your time, energy, hopes and dreams are all part of plan to make you happy, relaxed, and satisfied. It's not enough to choose a destination, buy a ticket, and build an itinerary. Check references and get referrals before making arrangements. Don't give out your credit card information to strangers and keep your passport in a safe place. Unscrupulous people don't care how much they take from you. Don't let them steal the one thing that is truly priceless – your peace of mind.

Instant Identity Theft Kit

Protect Your Passport!

Have A Nice Trip, Don't Fall for A Scam!

NINE

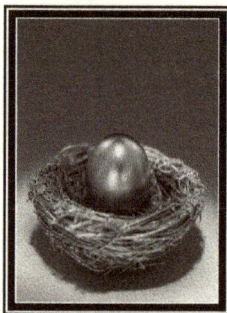

WINNERS AND LOSERS

Sweepstakes Swindles

Like most people I dream of hitting the lottery. I've mentally window-shopped and spent thousands of dollars of make-believe prize money and countless others have benefited in my dream world of riches. There are some real opportunities to win money and here's how it DOESN'T work.

After reading the directions carefully, you (hopeful contestant), fill in blanks, check the appropriate boxes, and then double check to be sure the information is correct, making a mental note of the drawing date. After all, you have just as good a chance as anyone else of winning the Grand Prize. Off the papers go into a mail carrier's vehicle, the stamp propelling your future chance at riches to its ultimate destination, the Publisher's Clearing House Sweepstakes office.

Imagine your delight when weeks later the telephone rings and an excited voice tells you that you are the winner of the Grand Prize in the Publisher's Clearing House sweepstakes! "In fact," the nice person continues, "I am here at the XYZ bank ready to deposit your winnings into your account. All I need is your bank account information, social security number, and date of birth and I will transfer the money right now!"

This is NOT, repeat NOT, how Publisher's Clearing House awards prizes. NO ONE EVER CALLS YOU ON THE PHONE. Sweepstakes prizes are actually awarded by the Prize Patrol as seen on television or a check is sent by mail. It is left to the discretion of the actual Prize Patrol as to when and how the money will be delivered. If done by mail, a letter accompanies the check and verification is simple.

Publisher's Clearing House is aware that their name is used in dishonest ways. In other instances people have received phone calls stating they have been awarded the Grand Prize because the first person chosen was found to be a terrorist! Publisher's Clearing House is very pro-active in trying to stop scammers using the PCH name. They want to hear from anyone who has had a problem or who has received a call from someone claiming to be one of their employees. Their customer service number is **1-800-459-4724** and their website is http://www.pch.com./. Helpful representatives will take some basic information from you and assist in the complaint process. They also may refer you to the Federal Trade Commission. Their toll-free number is **1-877-382-4357** or visit the website at www.ftc.gov. Both organizations are there to help.

Variations on sweepstakes scams include requests to wire money as an advance fee for collecting your prize or a "Sweepstakes Headquarters" sends a bogus check through the mail with instructions to cash it and wire back the necessary processing fees. Not only will you have to repay your bank for the fake check, you may face criminal charges for cashing it in the first place. It's important to remember that just because someone calls you, or you receive an official looking envelope or email, it doesn't mean the prize offer is genuine. Think things through before you act and don't give out bank account numbers or any other personal information. If you've been approached by a sweepstakes swindler, you can file a complaint by calling the FTC toll-free **1-877-382-4357**. By helping yourself you can truly help others, and for many that is their winning ticket.

Real Deal or Scam to Steal?

TEN

FACT OR FICTION

Stranger Danger on the Phone

New scams are popping up faster than kernels of corn in a crowded movie theatre. Dishonest strangers concoct wild stories worthy of Oscar nominations for deceit and seasoned cons earn a place in the faker category for pretending to be legitimate telemarketers using real scripts and lines. The storytelling and characters are all part of an effort to steal from unsuspecting consumers and here's how the tale unwinds.

The phone rings and a pleasant voice starts a conversation by introducing themselves as Mr./ Mrs./Ms. Doe and proceeds to tell you that they are calling from the Security and Fraud Department because your credit card has been flagged for an unusual purchase pattern. The caller then asks if you have made a recent purchase of a "Great Item" for $497 from the ABC Company located in "Somewhere USA". "No," you answer, concerned and confused. "Let me verify your address." She/he recites your correct address and you confirm.

"We'll be opening a Fraud investigation. If you have any questions please call the toll-free number on the back of your credit card. Your special control number is 12345. Before we end our conversation I need to verify that you are in possession of your card. Please turn your card over and look for 7 numbers. The first 4 are part of your card number and the last 3 are security numbers. Please read the last 3 numbers to me so that I can make note of the fact that you are in possession of your card." You comply, grateful that a crime has been averted and your account has been saved. Or has it?

Further investigation reveals that within 20 minutes of hanging up, $497 worth of items were charged to that person's account using the last 3 digits on the card. The customer called the 800 number on the back of the card to ask a question and spoke with the REAL Security and Fraud Department and was informed that credit card companies never call and ask for that type of information. They issued the card and have all the details they need! A REAL complaint was made, a legitimate credit was applied, the card was cancelled, and a new account number was issued. The customer learned the hard way that not all fiction is in books.

Another variation on this type of scam is the "Can you hear me" call. The caller will ask if you can hear them and then records your *yes* reply to use for fraudulent phone purchases. If disputed, the company has your actual voice on file and it is difficult to prove it wasn't you who made the purchase.

The "grandparent scam" continues to make its way around the country. It starts with a frightening call in the middle of the night from someone claiming to be a grandchild or friend of a grandchild calling about an accident or urgent problem. They plead for money and give instructions on how and where to send it. Unsuspecting folks send the money immediately only to find out it was a scam. Set up a special code word with loved ones to stop these callers in their tracks!

Con artists make their living preying on unsuspecting folks. Don't assume that the person on the telephone asking for personal information should have it. Take the initiative and do your own investigation. Read your credit card statements each month. If YOU make a call and are asked questions by a reputable business, then it's okay to proceed. Ask your own questions and when in doubt, don't give it out. You don't need to be a Hollywood director to have a happy ending. When approached by strangers looking for personal information, write your own script and stick with it. Just say NO.

Phone-y Fables and Scamming Tales

ELEVEN

DEBIT OR CREDIT

Automatic Debiting and How It Works

"Congratulations on the purchase of your 2013 Brand New Car," the voice chirps when you pick up the phone.

"I'm sorry, you must have the wrong number," you answer politely.

"Oh, aren't you Mr. /Mrs. /Ms. XXX?"

"Yes, I am. But I haven't purchased a 2017 Brand New Car. There must be some mistake."

"Okay. No problem. Could you please read me the numbers from the bottom of one of your checks and verify your date of birth? We'll get this taken care of right away."

This scenario and similar ones take place frequently as dishonest telemarketers devise more schemes to deceive honest people. One might assume that no real damage can be done with just a checking account number. Besides, checks require signatures, your banker knows you fairly well, and the whole incident was a mistake anyway. But, a false sense of security can lead to real trouble.

Devious scammers can wipe out your bank account with ease. After getting your checking account information they can submit a "demand draft" which is processed much like a regular check. The difference is that your signature is NOT needed on a demand draft. The money flows out of your account and into their pockets. All it took was a pleasant voice and your cooperation.

Automatic debiting of your checking account can be a legitimate way to pay some of your bills. However, there are certain legal requirements an institution or business must follow when debiting your account on a regular basis. Written or tape-recorded authorizations have to be given before any transactions take place and must include the following : date of the draft, the amount, payor's name (who is receiving the money), the number of payments needed to pay the debt, a legitimate phone number you can call during regular business hours, and the date you want the payments debited from your account. In addition, refund instructions must be clearly stated in case a dispute arises.

Guard your checking account information as you would your social security number, credit cards, and any other personal information. Do not give out bank account information unless YOU have agreed to a particular method of payment and are sure the business is reputable. Check all bank statements to be sure there are no unauthorized withdrawals and make note of your balances and payments. Contact your bank immediately if you believe you've been a victim of unauthorized debiting and follow their instructions for correcting the problem. Additional information is available by calling CFPB (Consumer Financial Protection Bureau) at **1-855-411-2372** or visit www.consumerfinance.gov.

By now many consumers have received new credit cards embedded with a chip designed to cut down on fraudulent transactions. EMV cards (Europay, MasterCard, and Visa) generate a random number for each transaction and customers have an extra added layer of protection when they shop using "chip and dip" technology. As with any new advancements and/or improvements, scammers are taking advantage new credit cards.

Imposters are sending out emails phishing for personal information by claiming that the credit card company is updating your account information and they provide a link "for your convenience" to check on your account details. Clicking on a phony link enables scammers to not only steal your valuable personal data, it also can install malware and/or viruses on your computer system. If you receive emails addressed to "Dear Cardholder" proceed with caution. Call your credit card company directly with any questions and take matters into your own hands.

Check Your Accounts

TWELVE

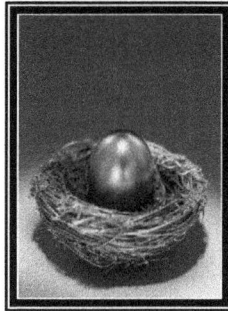

FOR FREE OR FOR A FEE

Offers Too Good To Be True

Lurking in the dark corners of mysterious messages and "special" offers are con artists and scammers trying to rip-off anyone who will listen to or read their rubbish. A popular and successful tactic is to use the word FREE when explaining great prizes, job opportunities, or advance loans that are available to you because you have been "specially" chosen to receive the great offers. The use of couriers, wire transfers, and prepaid cards like Green Dot MoneyPak should cause a warning bell to ring in your head because "free" suddenly becomes "fee" and it isn't a typo.

Frugal shoppers often fill out coupons for extra savings or enter their names for drawings, hoping to win a grand prize. Malls are a great place to take a chance at winning something. In reality, many forms include tiny statements allowing your name, address, and phone numbers to be added to telemarketing lists. By signing or filling out the papers you have inadvertently given permission to be called by salespeople trying to make deals over the phone. Read grocery coupons carefully. A free six-pack of soda may cost you in other unexpected ways.

Fraudulent telemarketers can be very convincing. They might inform you that you've won a free prize but state that you must pay the taxes and shipping fees before you can claim it. Using a courier might speed things up, they add, but once anything has been sent via courier, it's gone. No money, no shipping, no prize.

Another scheme is online job applications posted on bogus websites. Unsuspecting job seekers fill out forms and hope to be selected for positions that sound great. Imagine the joy when an applicant receives an email telling them they've been hired with instructions to wire a small fee for a background check and a company uniform prior to the first work day. Eager to work, many people wire money only to find no job exists and neither does the company. The fake sites are taken down and a similar scam pops up under a different name but with the same intent.

During troubling economic times many people have difficulty making ends meet. Con artists know that and invent ways to steal from others to pay their own bills. One easy way to access additional funds is applying for advance fee loans. An example is the "free" pre-approved notices that promise to lend money. However, the lender requires up-front payments so the borrowers can "prove" they are acting in good faith. One of the newer methods of payment is called a Green Dot MoneyPak. Consumers purchase a card for just under $5.00 and load it with cash at a local retailer or via credit card online. The "lender" then asks for the serial number printed on the card in order to access your funds and withdraw whatever amount they claim is due. In reality the customer has just given a stranger complete access to ALL of the funds in the account which are then deposited directly into the scammer's nest egg, never to be seen again. Green Dot MoneyPak is not liable for stolen money. They strongly advise customers not to give out serial numbers over the phone or online and suggest transferring money into a PayPal account as a safe way to make any type of payments. Additional suggestions can be found on their website at www.greendot.com or call **1-866-795-7597.**.

There is wealth and valuable wisdom that can be shared when we observe our own activities. Whether free or for a fee, make sure you don't pay too high a price for your decisions.

Free Deal or Another Way to Steal?

THIRTEEN

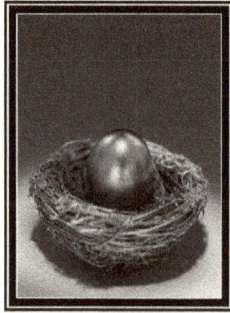

SEARCH FOR REPUTABLE RESOURCES

Better Business Bureaus

If you're like most people looking for service, skimming through ads and directories can be time-consuming and confusing. Who does what, are they reputable, and are they dependable are a few questions that come to mind. One detail that seems to put people at ease is a business with membership in the Better Business Bureau, also known as the **BBB.** It's a sign of trust and reliability.

Founded in 1912, the primary goal of the Better Business Bureau was to nurture positive, reliable relationships between businesses and clients. Contrary to popular belief, Better Business Bureaus are not government entities and they don't have any legal authority over commercial enterprises. They are, in fact, private, non-profit organizations that are funded not only with membership dues, but also by contributions from local businesses. A local Chamber of Commerce works in a somewhat similar fashion.

The Council of Better Business Bureaus oversees the **BBB** system. Each location keeps information gathered from several sources to help assist consumers and businesses alike. Their ultimate goal is to act as an impartial mediator in disputes and to help find resolutions when problems arise. For example, if Customer #1 has a grievance against Business #2, the **BBB** will contact the business and work towards an acceptable solution to the complaint. However, Business #2 is not legally bound to respond and, if they refuse, it's noted in a business review which is made available to the public. Most companies cooperate and work towards amicable solutions.

Business reviews contain descriptions and details about a company such as complaints processed over a certain period of time, names of principal officers, and other pertinent information that relates to their reputation and standing within the business community. The reports are made available to the public and contain only government actions that are based on alleged violations of laws or regulations. Private matters are civil in nature and are not recorded because they have no legal foundation as backgrounds to the complaints.

A local Chamber of Commerce compiles lists and directories of small businesses and professional firms to distribute to members and others who seek information about a community. Their primary goal is to promote businesses and provide programs to help stimulate the local economy. Some of their services include counseling for small businesses, providing materials to visitors and/or newcomers, and community projects geared towards increasing interest in local enterprises. Members pay a fee to be listed in directories and anyone can join. There are no prerequisites or special criteria for enrollment.

Advancements in technology have made it easier for us to investigate and research options before making important decisions. Each state has a website designed to answer queries about licensing, laws, and other legitimate concerns facing citizens at one time or another. Go to www.bbb.org for more tips on how to stay informed.

It's not enough anymore to rely on pieces of paper or ads in newspapers when shopping for services. Scammers and con artists are everywhere planning and scheming to take advantage of people every chance they get. Taking care of business isn't just for owners. It applies to you, too!

The Three "R"s – Read, Research, and Review

FOURTEEN

THE NUMBERS GAME

Personalized "Do Not Call" List

No matter who or where you are, we've all probably shared a common annoyance. Just as you get ready to rest your head on a soft pillow or sit to share a meal, the phone rings and somebody, somewhere, tries to sell you something you don't need. Telemarketers have an uncanny knack for calling at the worst possible times. Many people have already registered their numbers with the National Do Not Call Registry (**1-888-382-**

1222), but if it's been 5 years or more, you may need to re-register. There is no charge to be added to the list and you can include your cell phone number (s). Be sure to call the toll-free number from the phone you wish to add, or register online at www.donotcall.gov. An important detail regarding Robocalls! The Do Not Call list cannot prevent robocalls because they are computer-generated and are able to bypass any restrictions or notifications with specialized software. You may be able to block calls with your carrier and/or apps on your phone.

Another precaution consumers can take is to set up personalized Do Not Call lists to protect themselves from scams that add unauthorized charges to phone bills and unwanted callers on the phone. Most 800 and 888 numbers are free, but not all numbers beginning with an "8" are. For example, an 809 area code connects you to the Dominican Republic, an 876 area code connects you to Jamaica, and an 868 area code is for Trinidad. The numbers appear to be domestic calls but are, in fact, international numbers and you will be charged accordingly.

Scammers use several tactics to try to lure you into calling their trick numbers. Ever receive a message asking if there is a problem with your credit, or saying you have won a special gift, or a family member has been injured? The return call you make can actually be an international call and you end up speaking with a seasoned pro waiting to con you out of money. An example is the scammer who tries to keep you on the line for as long as possible. She/he earns money by receiving a portion of the long distance charges when the foreign companies add additional charges to your regular phone bill. The company is outside of the U.S. jurisdiction so there is no recourse once the bill is issued.

In addition to setting up your own Do Not Call List, check your phone bills each month and be sure the charges are valid. If not, notify your carrier. Oftentimes they will give you credit for calls you didn't make. If you are unsure of an area code, check the telephone directory which lists all area codes in the front of the book. Cell phone users should be wary, too, as they could be billed for roaming fees and other charges in addition to wasting valuable airtime speaking with bogus callers. Whether high-pressure or overly friendly, rip-off artists try to gain your trust and keep you talking until they get what they want. Never give out personal information or credit card numbers and don't hang on. Hang up!

Don't Count on Strange Numbers

PART 3

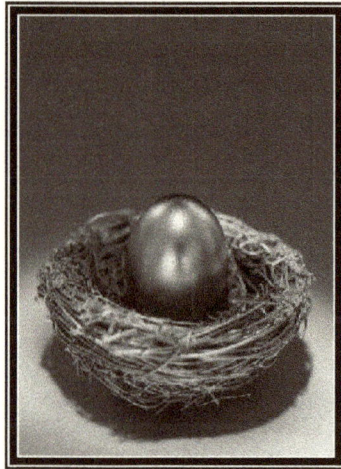

COMPUTER CONS AND CONSEQUENCES

SCAMMUNITION

FIFTEEN

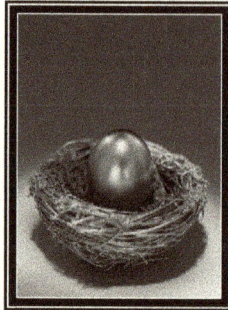

SELLER BEWARE

Suggestions For Online Sellers

If you're like me, Spring is the best time to clean out my garage, spruce up lawn furniture, and maybe find all those things that I put in a "safe place", the secret location I no longer remember, but stumble across when I least expect it. Here are some safe cleaning tips I try to follow no matter the season.

Suppose you've found an old laptop gathering dust in the

corner of a closet and you decide to sell it. After much thought and a little research, you decide on an asking price, jot a description on a piece of paper, and place an ad online. After several days someone expresses interest in your great deal. Under different circumstances it would be time for the *buyer* to beware, but in this instance it is *seller* beware. Not only does the *buyer* want your item, he or she will pay MORE than the asking price. This is not a dream come true, it is a nightmare in the making!

Let's assume the selling price is $200. *Buyer* offers $275, an agreement is reached in cyberspace, and *seller* checks the mail everyday waiting for a money order to arrive so the computer can be packed up and shipped off. The envelope arrives, but there's a slight problem. The money order is for $975, not $275, and communication with the *buyer* is imperative because of the huge discrepancy. Emails fly back and forth, the error is addressed, and the matter seems resolved. The *buyer* explanation is that her cousin made a mistake and sent the wrong money order to you. She then asks you to deposit the full amount, $975, into your personal bank account, and then purchase a new money order for $700, the difference in the amount you are owed and the wrong amount received, and then send it to John Doe in Kokomo who is awaiting his payment just like you were.

Off to the bank where the money order for $975 is deposited, a cashier's check for $700 is issued, and the envelope is mailed right away to the patient party who *buyer* has designated as the rightful owner of $700. After the laptop is packed, the box is taped, labels are filled out, and the package is off on its journey to the new owner.

Meanwhile, unbeknownst to you, the bank has discovered the money order you cashed is counterfeit and they are now considering legal action against you for fraudulently cashing an illegal document! Frantic emails to *buyer* go unanswered and an investigation reveals the address for John Doe is a rented mailbox space that has recently been closed for non-payment of fees. The situation becomes worse when YOU are held accountable for the full $975 because an unknown cyber-con duped you by using your own information placed in a classified ad.

Scam artists lie in person, on the phone, and online where being anonymous can be a curse instead of a blessing. Common sense is often the best weapon against thieves and cons. Stop and think for a moment. Unless an item is a valuable collector's piece, why would someone offer to pay MORE than what you are asking? Would you pay MORE for an item than what it is worth? Why put your trust in an invisible entity on a computer screen? Use caution on Craigslist and other similar sites. Be leery of meeting strangers in isolated places and use extreme caution in all dealings with questionable sources. Sometimes MORE is actually LESS – less trustworthy, less dependable, and less than honest. Safety, honesty, and integrity are the real deals, and they don't cost a thing.

Are They Paying or Playing?

SIXTEEN

CYBER SHAMS AND SCAMS

No Rules For Playing Fair

I love words and truly enjoy the sounds and meanings in our language. I've found it very interesting to watch technology change the landscape of how and why we do things and actually redefine some of the vocabulary we use every day. In the not so distant past "Password" was a television game show, "Spam" was a food product, and "fishing" was a sport.

Today each word has a vastly different meaning. A password is needed for everything from bank accounts to home alarm systems, Spam is junk email, and "phishing" is deceptive email that tries to trick people into revealing valuable personal information. Another way to look at some of these issues is to use common sporting terms.

THE HOOK: You receive an offer from someone with a strange email address. It might say something like "Just saw your pic, you look great!" or "I've been looking for you!" Curious, you open the mail and read it. The words have "hooked" you. THE LINE: "You have been chosen", "We are updating our records", or "Your help is needed" are but a few of the lines used as bait. THE STINGER: As soon as you open the infected email or attachment, your personal information, including all email addresses, are sent directly to hackers who are now free to use the information in any way they please including sending the same email to everyone in your address book. They have made their "catch of the day" and you are it!

Like any sport or game, safeguards are needed and the use of proper tools and equipment are essential. First, delete any strange emails you receive. If you don't know the sender, don't open it. Next, if something pops up or opens on its own, hit the X in the corner to close and delete it. Many email programs allow you to screen senders and if a name is not on your list, the mail never reaches your inbox. It's also possible to block people you no longer wish to communicate with.

A crucial component of any computer system is current anti-virus software and regular scans which automatically check for updates and installs them. Users can choose convenient times to run scans on a regular basis and eliminate any potential problems.

Another way hackers and scammers try to get your attention is with official looking emails claiming to be from companies you actually use. As an example, no Internet Service Provider (ISP) ever asks for your password, social security number, or credit card number. Your bank already has your information and so do the credit card companies you do business with. Free trips and prize offers should raise suspicion and requests for medical information from strangers should be dismissed entirely.

Please keep in mind that not all computers users have the same skills. Many are overwhelmed, frightened, and confused by ever-changing technology and evolving scams. Patience and understanding go a long way when trying to assist neighbors, friends, or family with on-going problems. Perhaps you can teach them some basic safety tips. Once someone gets caught hooked with a line, it may be too late to untangle the "nots" - not safe, not real, and not protected. Persistent problems can be reported to the FTC at www.ftc.gov or call toll-free **1-877-382-4357**. Remember, when in doubt, X it out and if an email is from someone unknown, hit delete, and leave it alone.

Cyber Care Keeps You Aware

SEVENTEEN

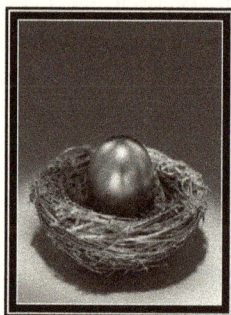

BE WARE - Y

Understanding Computer Terms

As technology advances, so does our need to keep up with the latest lingo. Most of us are familiar with terms like hardware, software, and shareware, but terms like spyware, scareware, and malware deserve our attention. It's not enough to know the words exist. We need a basic understanding of what they mean and how they apply to our own computer use. Here's another vocabulary lesson.

Spyware, like the name implies, secretly monitors your actions on the computer. It's hidden somewhere in your files and often hitchhikes a ride on a downloaded file keeping track of websites you visit, your buying preferences, and any other activities you may be involved in. Some spyware tries to gather personal information like passwords, bank account transactions, and credit card numbers. All spyware invades your privacy.

Scareware messages generate false warnings about your computer's security status. Similar to television commercials that interrupt favorite shows, scareware pops up and covers your screen with promotions and announcements that feed your fear of an imminent computer breakdown. Fake urgent messages claim to have solutions for infected software that they've supposedly found in your system or may include offers to improve the speed and capability of your existing system. The goal is to get you to purchase useless software so scammers can pocket your payments and rifle through personal information. Tech support scams work the same way. Mysterious callers offer assistance for your infected machine claiming to be a Microsoft technician who noticed you might have security issues. Hang up!

The word "malware" is a combination of two words, malicious and software. It is a catchall term used to describe software specifically written to destroy computers and/or networks. Examples include Trojan horses, viruses, and certain spyware. Trojan horse software is designed to damage or modify information on the hard drive and, in some instances, can retrieve personal information. It might appear to be useful to a user (like increasing the speed), but it can create a "backdoor" to your computer which allows hackers access to your system. Viruses, on the other hand, are a type of malware that spreads from one computer to another without your knowledge. They attach themselves to files or programs and once an infected file is sent to another computer user, it replicates and causes problems in that system as well. Some viruses lay dormant until a hidden trigger sets it off, then it opens and circulates.

In the last few months we've heard many stories about ransomware, a particularly nasty program that holds your computer "hostage." Officials advise against paying any ransom fees because there is no guarantee that your files will be returned or corrupted. Instead, they recommend keeping anti-virus software up to date, backing up files on a regular basis, and using caution before downloading attachments and apps.

It's hard to know what to expect when it comes to on-line piracy. Keeping track of new terminology is a step in the right direction. Be aWARE of cyber-attacks. BeWARE of strange emails and don't download items unless you are sure of their source. Protect yourself with anti-virus softWARE that finds and deletes destructive programs. It's the things you can't see that may hurt you when it comes to computers. Arming yourself with knowledge may be your best defense.

Got A DictionWAREy?

EIGHTEEN

PHISHING, PHARMING,
AND FRAUD

Phony Sites and Infected Bytes

Assume, for a moment, that you want to visit a favorite web
page where you've shopped before. You enter the URL
(universal resource locator aka web address), and a DNS
(domain name system) server turns the alphabet symbols into
numbers and directs your browser to the site you've chosen.
The change takes place in seconds inside your computer and
the website appears to be what you are looking for, but is it?
"Phishing" and "pharming" are two terms that describe the

deliberate misuse and manipulation of web addresses and sites for the purpose of stealing personal data and infiltrating your computer system to cause further harm.

Suppose the familiar colors and logos of a well-known business fill your computer screen when you click a button. In a world of impersonal transactions, an email thanking you for being a valued customer may seem like an anomaly rather than a customary gesture. Finally, you think, my years as a loyal customer counts for something. The special limited time offer of a free gift catches your eye. The only requirement is that you fill in your account information on a form "for verification purposes" so your reward can be sent as soon as possible. Clicking that link sends your information into cyberspace and a "phishing" expedition has been successful.

Closely related to "phishing" is "pharming", a carefully crafted viral attack on a computer system that reroutes your website selections to a fake site without your knowledge. "Pharming" (not to be confused with genetic farming), enables a "pharmer" to spoof a domain by making it look exactly like the legitimate site. Malicious codes then redirect the browser to an illegal website without the user's knowledge. Phony banking sites are popular in this type of scam and the fake sites are taken down after a few days to avoid detection and discovery by authorities.

When the Internet was first developed its purpose was to exchange facts and ideas in a very efficient way. Financial transactions were not the focus of the system and safeguards weren't automatically built into programs. As technology progressed and demand grew, banks and other commercial institutions became part of the network and advanced security measures were developed as scammers and hackers devised new ways to steal and cheat. Many banking services have now added multi-step security features like encryption, verification programs, and explicit password instructions which all add an additional layer of protection.

Some suggestions for safety include staying informed about new security features. Be being leery of pop-up ads and sales pitches with special links that claim to offer more of whatever you are looking for. When shopping online look for the **S** in the web address, **https//** (not http//), and a padlock icon in the toolbar which means the site is secure and safe to use. Updated anti-virus and anti-spyware software is essential and so is careful observation. In a world full of whirring gadgets it is easy to forget that sometimes the best processor of all is the human brain. Be sure to use it!

Phishing Isn't Phun!

NINETEEN

HO HO HELP

Harried Holidaze

There's a collective sigh of relief when the holidaze are over. Decorations and lights are nestled in their respective containers lying dormant until next year's festivities. Boxes have been opened, manuals have been read, and a blitz of directions rumble through weary brains amidst the noise of bells, whistles, and hoots coming from new electronic gadgets. Gone are the days when a hammer and screwdriver were all that were needed to bring gifts to life. Today we need lithium batteries, car chargers, home chargers, headsets, laptops, tablets, and E-Readers not to mention LCD's, HD, USBs, CDs, and DVDs. It's enough to make a person want to scream HELP, but even that will cause six more windows to drop down on a screen somewhere displaying an array of choices that you've already considered in the first place. Tired, frustrated, and confused, many people stumble off to bed and mumble meaningless phrases in their sleep about ports, serials, and processors, none of which have anything to do with food. Rather than add to the confusion, here are a few simple safety reminders.

COMPUTERS: Do not give out your personal information in response to strange email requests. Keep your virus protection software updated and use it regularly. X out any unknown emails in your inbox and do not store all your passwords and confidential information on your computer. Guard against cyber-creeps.

CELL PHONES: If you are thinking about a new cell phone carrier, be sure to stop and start a new account at the end of your billing cycle. Big carriers don't prorate when you switch and will charge for a full month of coverage no matter where you are in your billing cycle. Avoid paying for both the old and new services when you change carriers. Also remember to add your new cell phone to the Do Not Call Registry by calling **1-888-382-1222** from the phone you wish to register or register online at http://donotcall.gov/.

WARRANTY CARDS: Many forms ask for private information which is used for marketing purposes and has nothing to do with the actual product you have purchased. When filling out warranty cards provide necessary information only such as name, address, model #, and any product identification codes needed to identify the product. Recall notices are usually sent via postcard or letter to the address given on a warranty card. Any additional unnecessary data can be sold and used for telemarketing purposes.

SAFETY/RECALLS: If you are concerned about product safety issues, recall notices, or other problems please contact:

Consumer Product Safety Commission (CPSC)
1-800-638-2772 www.cpsc.gov
Food and Drug Administration
1-888-463-6332 www.fda.gov
U.S. Postal Service
1-800-275-8777 www.usps.com

If all else fails, remember others may be navigating through a maze of manuals just like you. Sometimes old-fashioned face to face conversations can help solve problems better than any machines. You may make a new friend and that's a great gift to yourself.

Help*#@&!

TWENTY

SPECIAL DELIVERIES

What's in the Box?

Most of us would agree that it's fun to receive packages in the mail. We check the wrapping, shake boxes gently, and open with care so the contents aren't damaged or disturbed. We also sprinkle Styrofoam nuggets or use bubble wrap and newspaper to cushion special items destined for another location and whether placed in a mailbox or hand-delivered by a driver, the efficiency and speed of delivery systems has changed. Transactions are completed with the click of a button and confirmation emails allow us to follow the path of traveling merchandise. However, hidden in crammed inboxes disguised as official-looking receipts are bogus emails claiming to be from USPS, UPS, and/or FedEx and they are delivering major problems to unsuspecting recipients. If we take the time to examine physical boxes and envelopes, we need to be cautious about opening questionable messages from delivery companies and examine their contents with care.

Online advertising and choices in shipping options have changed our shopping opportunities and experiences. Shoppers can check prices and deals, use built-in scanners on phones and buy from specialized websites offering real bargains.   It would be easy to dismiss any delivery related emails from well-known companies if we didn't make any purchases, but family and friends might send surprise gifts and we have no control over that. Our postal carriers deliver mail six days a week and for the most part are familiar with customers on their routes. Why would the USPS send an email claiming to have problems with the delivery of an item when a note in your mailbox or a knock on the door would resolve any problem? Why would the USPS even have your email address under normal circumstances?

When using specialized delivery programs like UPS and FedEx, it's important to know that they follow strict guidelines and protocols. When items are shipped for delivery, tracking numbers are assigned to each parcel and given to the sender so that they can reference it if there are any questions or difficulties. Emails with attachments claiming to be from UPS and/or FedEx should NOT be opened. They contain viruses and malicious codes designed to infect and destroy computer systems. Neither company sends out attachments! If UPS uses email to notify someone of an issue, it is contained within the body of the email. If there is a legitimate problem with a package and delivery, both companies contact their local vendors who in turn contact the customer directly. The preferred mode for correspondence is a postcard in the mail with legitimate references and phone numbers included.

Neither company solicits additional money or personal account information in emails. They do not send out "urgent" requests or threatening letters nor do they use poor grammar and misspelled words.

If anyone receives impostor emails both companies have fraud departments that will investigate. If you have any questions call UPS at **1-800-742-5877** or visit their website at www.ups.com. For information on FedEx call **1-800-463-3339** or visit their website at www.fedex.com. Both are aware of the fraudulent activities of scammers and tracking can work in more ways than one.

Open With Care

PART 4

TRIPLE THREATS

SCAMMUNITION

TWENTY ONE

GIVE BUT DON'T BE TAKEN

Where Did the Money Go?

Disasters and accidents wreak havoc on so many different levels. One of the more despicable end results of devastation and destruction are cruel scam artists who prey on the generosity of caring people. Illegal "charities" suddenly appear in phone calls, emails, and even door-to-door solicitations complete with mock IDs. Once a donation is made to a phony fund, the money is gone and there is no recourse.

Unfortunately, the deception may not end once the contributions are collected.

Generous gestures can backfire when the charity you gave to is really a fake. A practice called "reloading" is used by fraudulent telemarketers to double scam donors. Once you have mistakenly given to a bogus organization, your name and phone number is placed on a "sucker list" and then sold to other dishonest telemarketers who operate on the assumption that you can be tricked again.

"Recovery room operators" use a "sucker list" to contact people who have already given to a fake charity or company. They offer to recover lost money or unclaimed prizes and will fill out special forms "FOR A FEE". Some never file your complaint while others charge ridiculous fees for providing names and addresses of government agencies that are readily available in the phone book and on-line.

If considering a donation to a charity, check them out first. before giving any money. Do they have an authentic address and phone number? Call the organization directly if you would like to make a contribution and ask if they are soliciting donations in whatever way you were approached. Never give a cash donation. It may end up in someone's pocket or be misplaced or lost. Is your donation tax deductible? Ask for a receipt and make sure the amount and term "tax deductible" is on it. Make your checks out to the organization and not the person collecting the donations or else he/she can cash the check and keep the money for personal use. Ask where and how are the funds disbursed? Do they have a valid tax I.D. number and are they "tax exempt" (pays no taxes)?

Check with the Better Business Bureau Wise Giving Alliance if you have questions regarding national charities. Visit www.give.org or call them at **703-247-9321**. Other resources include www.guidestar.org , www.charitywatch.org , and www.charitynavigator.org . It's great to be caring, but be careful as well.

Believing Can Be Deceiving

TWENTY TWO

MILITARY MANEUVERS

Preying on Patriotism

Holidays are a great time to celebrate. Generous people open their hearts and wallets so others can share in the joy of whatever the season brings. Many folks don't realize that scammers use patriotic celebrations like Memorial Day, Independence Day, and Veteran's Day to prey on military personnel and their families both here and abroad. Some of their targets include those on active duty, honest citizens trying to help those who protect our rights and freedom, and veterans who have already sacrificed enough.

Affordable housing is an area of concern for people currently serving our country. Frequent moves to different bases are stressful and time limitations can make apartment hunting difficult especially in areas like San Diego, CA, Biloxi, MS, and St. Augustine, FL. Scam artists tailor their online ads and newspaper listings with enticing phrases. "Military Discounts", "Special Military Rates", and "Reduced Rent for Military" are really disguises aimed at luring military families to their sites. While the property may sound promising, emails with bad grammar and vague details should set off alarms. Demands for money transfers and cashier's checks are warning signs of trouble. Many scammers pilfer information from sites like Craigslist and rent out apartments that are already rented or not for rent at all. Once any money is paid, there is no way to get it back. Check reputable sites like www.zillow.com for property information or the property appraiser website for that locale. Never commit to lease anything sight unseen!

A common ruse for selling a car is someone pretending to be a serviceman/woman who needs to sell their car quickly because they are being sent overseas. Pictures of gleaming autos and even videos convince many people that they are getting a great deal. Eager to help someone who is sacrificing personal freedom for their country, buyers wire money to the seller who promises the vehicle will be shipped for free upon receipt of the funds. Purchasers soon discover they've been duped when no vehicle arrives and their payment is used to take another victim for a ride. Conversely, if you are considering donating a car to a military charity, be sure it is going to a reputable organization and not to someone for their personal use.

Retired veterans are sometimes approached in person and by phone by impostors claiming to be VA employees. The "nice person" on the phone wants to assist with the application process for benefits and charges a "small fee" to get copies of a veteran's military records. In reality, there is no charge to veterans for their records and help is available for free by calling the Department of Veteran Affairs directly at **1-800-827-1000** or by visiting their website at www.va.gov. Stealing personal information is lucrative amongst thieves and the repercussions of identity theft can last for years. For more military consumer information visit the Better Business Bureau Military Line at www.military.bbb.org.

Many honest organizations reach out and help servicemen and women across the globe. With advancements in technology comes the real risk of cyber liars and clever cons. Check out any charities claiming to help members of the military before donating, don't take online ads at face value, and don't become a pawn in someone else's con. Our servicemen and women have given enough. Watching out for them is one small way to say thanks and welcome home.

Thanks to Those Who Have Given!

TWENTY THREE

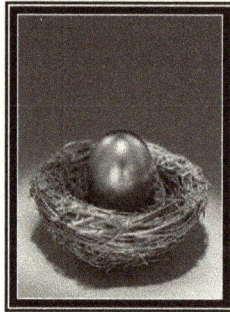

ANTI-SOCIAL MEDIA

Liking and Sharing Too Much

What would someone think of the following newspaper ad? Fully furnished, freshly painted, three-bedroom home available for immediate use. Features include comfortable furniture, free computer access and unlimited cable services and movies. Make lots of money and relax with designer clothing and gourmet goods delivered right to your door. Your dreams can come true! Get everything you've always wanted for free! The door key is under the mat at (insert address here). Help yourself to whatever you want while I'm away on vacation and have fun at my expense. Strangers and thieves are welcome! Friends and neighbors need not come by.

Sound silly or ludicrous? Unbelievable or unlikely? The same thing happens every day on *Facebook, Twitter, Instagram* and countless other social media sites when people post private information for everyone to see. There is a common misconception that social media is filled with honest friends and nice users who are looking to make connections with other cyber-socializers. Unlike other media, this type of communication has risks and security threats that can't be seen with the naked eye or be detected until after the damage is done. While cyber-circles are growing, hackers and scammers are invading computers, tablets, and smartphones like busy ants stealing food at a picnic, leaving viruses and worms behind long after their footprints are dusted away.

It's fairly easy for hackers to steal information from sites that promote friendship and sharing. There's nothing to stop someone from adopting an alias, altering or taking someone else's picture, and creating a super profile built on lies and deceit Information gleaned from accounts can be. used to send fake friend requests that are actually infected with viruses designed to steal personal data. Phony news items are planted to entice users to click on a link which allows hackers to gather even more info about loved ones and friends via your social media posts and interests. For security issues or concerns visit the Privacy/Security/Help sections for each site.

Smartphones and cell phones are not immune to attacks. With more people choosing to text rather than talk, phone phishing has become profitable for opportunists and cons. Unexpected texts say you have won a gift card and includes instructions on how to claim it. Filling out your name and address may not seem risky, but once the scammer on the other end has your reply , they have determined that your phone has a working number and they can then sell your details to another devious texter. To assist with unwanted texts, many carriers have set up a special "text 7726" program to try to stem the flow of harmful messages. Check with your cell phone company to see if it is available in your area.

Technology is changing every day and the scammers and con artists in the world are keeping up with each new enhancement. They have no morals, prey on innocent people, and hide behind a wall of digital deception. If we are going to use computerized accessories, we need to program ourselves to be safety-literate. Pay attention to small details, use common sense, and if in doubt, throw it out. You, the human being, can use your own mind and you don't need an app for that!

TMI (Too Much Information)!

SCAMMUNITION

PART 5

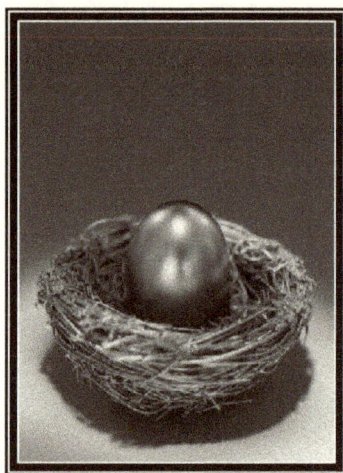

IDENTITY MATTERS

TWENTY FOUR

WHO ARE YOU?

Identity Theft

In an age where cell phones and tablets stream movies and emails and texts have replaced handwritten letters, it would seem that guarding personal data should be as simple as pushing a privacy button hidden somewhere amongst all the electronic devices throughout our homes. In fact, the opposite is true. Never before have consumers been so vulnerable to privacy piracy as we are now. Identity theft is growing at a phenomenal rate and it's time to PYA (protect your assets). There is no single preventive measure to take when dealing with identity theft issues. It's more a series of careful maneuvers designed to increase your awareness of the problem and decrease your susceptibility to becoming an unwitting victim.

Identity thieves extract personal information in several ways. For example, bogus emails from reputable looking sites request passwords, credit card, and bank account verifications, even threatening to suspend current activities if you do not comply. Do NOT give out the information! Legitimate companies never ask you to respond to queries about passwords and financial information, and they don't use vague threats. If you have concerns or questions call the company directly and mention the email. Corporate offices do monitor illegal activities using their names or logos and appreciate any reports they receive.

SHRED! SHRED! SHRED! Get in the habit of shredding unwanted paperwork, especially unsolicited applications for credit cards, offers to lower your APR, and anything that asks for your personal information. Determined thieves actually "dumpster dive" to retrieve that discarded mail, fill out the forms, and pretend to be you. Rented mailboxes serve as your new address and a whole new person, credit history, and spending spree is started using tattered papers found in barrels and landfills. Shredders are inexpensive, easy to use, and take very little time. A small investment allows you to be pro-active in the fight against identity theft. No shredder? Use scissors. No scissors? Tear it up. No time? No excuses!

If you would like to stop receiving credit card and insurance solicitations in the mail, call **1-888-5-OPTOUT** (**1-888-567-8688**) or visit www.optoutprescreen.com. Because the three credit reporting agencies are part of the program, representatives will ask for your Social Security number. Keep in mind the fact that YOU initiated the call and are requesting services and, in this instance, the credit agencies already have your SSN and need it to prescreen your removal request. To be removed from catalog or other marketing lists visit www.DMAchoice.org.Their mailing address, should you choose to write:

DMA POB 900 Cos Cob CT 06807

A great free safeguard is to order your own credit reports at least once a year. Is the spelling of your name correct? ID thieves may apply for credit using a slight variation of your name using your actual credit history. Consumers are now entitled to one *free* credit report per year. For more information call **1-877-322-8228** or log on to www.annualcreditreport.com the Annual Credit Report Request Form is received, fill out and mail to:

Annual Credit Report Request Service
POB 105281
Atlanta GA 30348-5281

Once received check the reports carefully for the following information to be sure it is accurate.

Is your personal information correct (birthdate, SS#, etc.)?
Are there any unfamiliar accounts listed?
Is there any incorrect information listed?

If there are discrepancies, contact the credit bureaus to get the data corrected.

Equifax: www.equifax.com
1-800-685-1111

Experian: www.experian.com
1-888-397-3742

TransUnion: www.transunion.com
1-888-909-8872

Who is Preying on You?

TWENTY FIVE

MEDICAL IDENTITY THEFT

COVID-19 Scams and More

Medical Identity Theft is on the rise and it is crucial to be vigilant with your personal medical information. Con artists try to use your data for many reasons including obtaining prescription drugs for resale in an illegal market, claiming benefits and treatments using your name, and selling your card numbers to others who will use your name to commit more fraud. New Medicare cards were issued in April 2018 using random digits as identifiers. The goal is to protect your identity and reduce fraudulent activities. In the meantime be sure to monitor all Explanation of Benefits forms you receive and don't lend your insurance card to anyone. Shred any medical documents when no longer needed and guard your information when at your doctor's office. Medicare never calls you for information or to offer you special discounts for products such as knee and back braces or fake DNA tests to help you discover any hidden health deficiencies. For any discrepancies or questions call Medicare at 1-800-633-4227.

As soon as *COVID-19* began to wreak havoc on everyone's lives scammers concocted hundreds of schemes to take advantage of people's fears and vulnerabilities. Whether by phone, online, or in person they spread their tentacles of deceit into a confusing situation to prey on everyone especially homebound seniors. As uncertainty and global fears rose scammers continued to adapt their tactics and lies. Once vaccines became available a whole new wave of fake offers and claims became available via social media and other means. Here are some tips to protect yourself and loved ones when it comes to *COVID-19.* Of note is the fact that Medical Identity Theft and *COVID-19* scams both have the same intent to steal your info!

Do NOT pay to make an appointment for a vaccine. There is no cost to sign up for the vaccine and there are no "early" testing spots available to anyone.
Do NOT pay for shot if you are on Medicare and it is NOT available for purchase no matter what an ad may say.
Vaccination cards should NOT be shared on social media and are not for sale. Posting photos of vaccination info is an invitation to scammers to use your data for Identity Theft.
Medicare does NOT call you to offer any *COVID-19* products or services and does not solicit your personal health status.

Be aware that there are NO free at-home tests kits, no miracle cures, and no special products to eliminate the virus.

Pay attention to updates from reputable resources. Here are a few sites that offer information and more *COVID-19* safety tips.

Federal Trade Commission www.ftc.gov/coronavirus/scams 1-877-382-4357 File complaint www.ftc.gov/complaint

Local resources visit www.usa.gov/coronavirus

Internal Revenue Service : www.IRS.gov/coronavirus

Federal Drug Administration: www.fda.gov

Centers for Disease Control: www.cdc.gov

It is easy to be lulled into a false sense of security. Beepers, bells, and whistles all serve as warning signs of imminent danger, but there is no uniform way to safeguard identities. Consumers need to use their own safety plans. After all, who you are on paper is just as important as who you are in person. Both should be treated with care.

COLLEEN J. PALLAMARY

APPENDIX

Additional Consumer Resources

Please Note: Websites and Addresses May Change Without Warning. Author has listed most recent as of this writing.

FEDERAL AND STATE AGENCIES

ADDITIONAL RESOURCES

AARP
www.aarp.org
1-888-687-2277

Better Business Bureau
www.bbb.org
1-703-276-0100

Consumer Action
www.consumer-action.org
1-415-777-9635

Consumer Federation of America
www.consumerfed.org
1-202-387-6121

Consumer Financial Protection Bureau
www.consumerfinance.gov
1-855-411-2372

Credit Bureaus
Experian www.experian.com 1-888-397-3742
Equifax www.equifax.com 1-888-648-7878
TransUnion www.transunion.com 1-855-681-3196

Department of Homeland Security
www.dhs.gov

Department of Veterans Affairs
www.va.gov
1-800-827-1000

Eldercare Locator
www.eldercare.acl.gov
1-800-677-1116

Federal Citizen Information Center
www.usa.gov
Various State and Federal listings

Federal Communications Commission
www.fcc.gov
1-888-225-5322

Federal Trade Commission (FTC)
www.ftc.gov
1-202-326-2222

Federal Express
www.fedex.com
1-800-463-3339

Funeral Information

Cremation Assoc. of North America
www.cremationassociation.org
1-312-245-1077

Funeral Consumers Alliance
www.funerals.org
Toll free: 1-802-865-8300

Funeral Ethics Organization
www.funeralethics.org
1-802-482-6021

Green Burial Council
www.greenburialcouncil.org
1-888-966-3330

International Cemetery, Cremation, and Funeral Assoc
www.iccfa.com
1-800-645-7700

National Funeral Directors Association
www.nfda.org
 1-800-228-6332

Identity Theft Resource Center
www.idtheftcenter.org

Internal Revenue Service
www.irs.gov
1-800-829-1040

National Assoc. of Attorneys General
List of AG for each state
www.naag.org
1-202-326-6000

National Assoc. Consumer Advocates

Senior Medicare Patrol National Resource Center
www.smpresource.org
1-877-808-2468

US Consumer Safety Commission
www.saferproducts.gov
1-800-638-2772

US Food and Drug Administration
www.fda.gov
1-888-463-6332

US Social Security Administration
www.ssa.gov
1-800-772-1213

UPS
www.ups.com
1-888-742-5877

US Postal Service
www.usps.com
1-800-275-8777

NOTES